MW01236366

U.S. Presidents & Their Animal Friends

Jacquelyn Autrey 2004

Written by Jacquelyn Autrey and Alice Yeager
Illustrated by Jennie Passarella

To: Ms. Smith,
Animal lovers are special people!

Published by Seacoast Publishing, Inc.
1149 Mountain Oaks Drive
Birmingham, Alabama 35226

Copyright © 2004 Jacquelyn Autrey and Alice Yeager

Printed in China.

Library of Congress Control Number: 2003115978

ISBN 1-59421-005-5

To obtain copies of this book, please write or call:
Seacoast Publishing, Inc.
Post Office Box 26492
Birmingham, Alabama 35260
(205) 979-2909
seacoast@charter.net

Imagine you've just become President of the United States — that'll take a pretty big imagination — but you can do it!

You pack up most of your belongings and move to 1600 Pennsylvania Avenue in Washington, D.C. Instantly you become the busiest person in America. Almost every single day you travel throughout the country or even the world. You are in charge of making major decisions all day long and people continuously demand your time and attention. How in the world are you going to keep your sanity?

Maybe you'll do what almost every other president has done . . . count on loyal animal friends to help you.

Many, many pets have lived at the White House. These furry and feathery (and even scaly) creatures have been a very important part of the lives of our country's famous First Families.

Of course you know that George Washington was our very first President. He became President before the White House was built but there were several special pets at his home in Virginia.

The Father of our Country lived on a large plantation called Mount Vernon. The plantation was home to the usual farm animals, along with the President's hunting dogs. A favorite dog named Vulcan sneaked into the smokehouse and grabbed a ham — he gobbled up the entire ham before anyone could stop him! George Washington also thought highly of his riding horse. Nelson was a large white horse and President Washington pampered the horse by keeping his hooves trimmed and painted black.

Martha Washington enjoyed her cats so much that she had a special door installed for them. Martha was also particularly fond of the family's pretty green parrot and she spent a lot of time teaching the little bird to sing.

President and Mrs. Washington were the first of many presidential families to love animals. Let's take a look at the animals that occupied a special place in the Presidents' homes and in their hearts throughout the years . . . cats, dogs, birds, horses . . . tigers, snakes, bears, and even alligators . . . can you believe that? Yes, these animals (plus others) have all lived in the White House or on its grounds. We'll begin with some furry friends that you may have at your house . . .

CATS

George and Martha Washington were not the only First Families that adored cats. Rutherford B. Hayes (1877-81) and his wife Lucy's love for animals quickly became recognized around the world. They were presented the first Siamese kitten to live in the United States. The little kitten arrived in America after a long sea voyage and immediately the President and his wife were crazy about "Siam."

Theodore Roosevelt (1901-1909) was a great lover of all animals. He had six children and kept many animals in and around the White House. One of their cats had six toes and was named Slippers. Slippers would get in one place, stretch out and absolutely refuse to be disturbed. Once President Roosevelt was leading a group of visiting dignitaries or important people around the White House. Slippers just happened to be sprawled out, sound asleep, and blocked their way. President Roosevelt paused a moment, bowed, and promptly led the lady he was escorting around the snoozing cat. Rather than disturb Slippers, all the others in the group stepped around the purring animal as well.

Bounder, Blackie, and Tiger were pet cats that belonged to Calvin Coolidge (1923-1929) and his wife Grace. President Coolidge liked to play with Bounder by hiding him in odd places. Sometimes Mrs. Coolidge would hear the very faint sounds of a crying cat. She would follow the sounds until she found Bounder – curled up inside some unusual place – even the Grandfather clock! Blackie the cat loved to ride the elevator and stood patiently in the hallway waiting for someone to open the door. Once inside, the cat curled up on the seat inside the elevator and stayed there for hours.

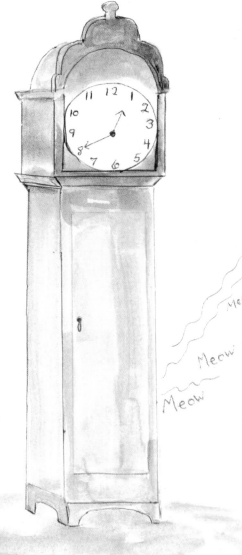

A cat named Socks became quite a celebrity during the Bill Clinton administration (1993 – 2001). Mrs. Clinton published a book about the family's furry black and white friend along with another family pet – Buddy the dog. Socks loved to pose for pictures and joined the Clintons as they visited hospitals, nursing homes, and orphanages. Socks had a special way of noticing when someone needed extra attention and he was always glad to make others feel better.

President George W. Bush and his wife Laura thought so highly of pets that the Christmas theme for 2002 was "White House Animals." Replicas of many of the presidential pets all through the years were displayed. President and Mrs. Bush moved to the White House with their cat named India. India "Willie" Bush likes to play hide-and-seek and her favorite place to hide is under the bed.

Just like many of us, the First Families have been crazy about cats – can you guess another furry resident that's been popular at the White House?

I bet you guessed it . . .

DOGS

Dogs and cats have probably been the most constant companions to our Presidents and their families. James Buchanan's (1857 – 1861) dog named Lara moved into the White House and was known for his total devotion to President Buchanan. Lara was a large, male Newfoundland with a gigantic tail and visitors to the White House marveled at Lara's ability to lie in one place, barely moving. The dog amazed everyone as he stretched out and rested with one eye open and one eye closed for hours at a time.

President Abraham Lincoln's (1861 – 1865) family had several pets during their stay at the White House, but Jip was known as the president's dog. Shortly before the president was assassinated, Jip sensed that something was terribly wrong. The little dog ran about the White House, wailing and howling uncontrollably. Dogs are like that you know — their love and devotion run deep!

If you visit the Smithsonian Institute in Washington, D.C., you will find a copper statue honoring President Warren Harding's (1921-1923) dog, Laddie Boy. Laddie Boy brought the newspaper to his master each morning and sat at the end of the breakfast table while nibbling food that President Harding "accidentally dropped."

The pampered dog went everywhere with the President, attending important meetings where a chair was always provided for him. He was even given a birthday party with a four-tier cake made of dog biscuits covered with white icing! Laddie Boy led the "Be Kind to Animals" parade while living at the White House. There were lots of floats, like "Mary's Lamb" and "Black Beauty," but Laddie Boy was everyone's favorite.

President Harding died while in office and newspaper boys throughout the country donated one penny each so that a famous artist could sculpt Laddie Boy's likeness. President Harding had served as a newspaper man before becoming President and the newspaper carriers gladly donated 19,134 pennies in his honor. The coins were melted down and used to create a replica of this famous animal that is displayed at the Smithsonian.

Laddie Boy's half brother (Laddie Buck) lived at the White House during the Calvin Coolidge administration (1923 – 1929). Mrs. Coolidge eventually changed his name to Paul Pry because he was so nosy — always sticking his nose in other people's business.

The Coolidge's had several other dogs while living in Washington. Mrs. Coolidge loved her dogs so much that she even invited them to the annual White House Easter Egg Rolling . . . each dog arrived wearing its very own elegant Easter bonnet!

Theodore Roosevelt's (1901 – 1909) family probably had the oddest assortment of pets – even their dogs were somewhat unusual. One of their dogs (Pete) had bitten so many people at the White House that he had to be sent to the family's home in Long Island. Alice Roosevelt's little Pekingese, (Manchu) was quite a dancer. Alice told others that one moonlit night she peeked out onto the White House lawn and watched her tiny black dog dancing on its hind legs – what a sight that must have been!

Would you believe that one dog has been credited with getting his master enough votes to become president? Herbert Hoover (1929 – 1933) didn't come across as a very friendly person and it looked as if the American public was not very impressed as he campaigned. Then a photo of Hoover and his canine companion, King Tut, appeared in newspapers. The photo captured a smiling candidate and his faithful friend . . . Hoover won enough votes to enter the White House.

President Hoover enjoyed sitting outside and reading the daily news. The faithful dog delivered the newspaper to his master each morning and King Tut often sprawled out on the papers to keep them from blowing away.

A small Scottish terrier named Fala was the constant companion of President Franklin Delano Roosevelt (1933 – 1945). Fala became well known and loved by the entire world. This small dog was quite an entertainer — he could sit up, roll over, jump and even curl his lips and smile at visitors. He slept each night in a special chair placed at the foot of the president's bed.

Almost every time you saw President Roosevelt, Fala was by his side. Once the little Scottish terrier was separated from his master while they were traveling together on a cruiser. Fala soon turned up, but he was missing quite a bit of fur. It seems that several of the sailors wanted some of the dog's fur for souvenirs!

President Roosevelt and Fala were extremely close. The greatly admired President died in April of 1945 at his home in Georgia just a short time after being elected to a fourth term. When President Roosevelt died, his tiny devoted friend immediately knew that something was wrong. Fala had been sitting quietly in the President's bedroom, but all of a sudden he ran from the room.

He busted through a screen door and ran to a hillside where he sat alone for hours.

Fala lived with Mrs. Roosevelt in the country for many more years. The little dog ran and romped for hours — sometimes he was so tired after playing that he slept on his back with his feet straight up in the air — can you imagine that?

Visitors to Washington, D.C. will notice a bronze statue of Fala sitting faithfully beside his master at the F.D.R. Memorial.

President John F. Kennedy (1961 – 1963) and his family had several pets while living in the White House. One of their dogs, Pushinka (meaning "fluffy" in Russian), gained a lot of attention when she was whisked off to Walter Reed Hospital. The public was told that the little dog was simply undergoing routine tests, but it was suspected that the animal was being searched for hidden microphones or bombs planted by the Russians. After all, she had been given to the Kennedy's by Soviet Premier Nikita Khrushchev. Pushinka's famous mother had been one of the first canines in space!

Lyndon Johnson (1963 – 1969) was criticized by the public after lifting his beagles named Him and Her by the ears. Johnson quickly told the public that beagles are "supposed to be picked up that way." Another canine member of the Johnson family was Yuki. Yuki was found at a gas station by President Johnson's daughter Luci. The president taught Yuki how to sing (or howl) and the two of them liked to entertain visitors to the White House. President Johnson would lean over and look out of the helicopter's window when landing back at the White House. He was always hoping that his devoted canine friends would be there to greet him.

A funny story is told about President Gerald Ford's (1974 – 1977) golden retriever named Liberty. One night the President was sleeping soundly when he was gently nudged out of bed by a cold nose. Liberty needed to go outside so the sleepy President led his canine friend to the White House lawn. When President Ford tried to get back in, he realized they were locked out. What a sight! The President of the United States locked outside in his pajamas!

President George Bush (1989 – 1993) and his wife Barbara enjoyed living with two rather famous canines. White House pets Millie and Fred became popular after writing autobiographies telling about life at the White House. In fact *Millie's Book* was one of the best selling books of its time. Millie even appeared on the cover of *Life* with her litter of puppies that were born at the White House.

President Bill Clinton (1993 – 2001) shared lots of happy times with his Labrador Retriever named Buddy. The chocolate Lab loved to splash and play in the fountain on the White House grounds and he was often seen sitting patiently outside the Oval Office waiting for his master. It was difficult to tell who was happier, President Clinton or Buddy when the two were reunited after the President had been away. Buddy proudly stood on his hind legs, placed his front paws on the President's chest, and gave lots of hugs and kisses. When President Clinton became bogged down in stressful work, he would take a break and play "fetch the ball" with his furry friend in the Rose Garden. This always helped the president relax.

George W. Bush and his family have a Scottish Terrier named Barney and an English Springer Spaniel named Spotty. Spotty's mother Millie lived in the White House when President Bush's father was President. Spotty is right at home in the White House – the little Spaniel sleeps on a chair in the First Couple's bedroom.

Along with cats and dogs — what other famous pets have lots of the Presidential families adored????

BIRDS

Many of the Presidents have shared their famous home with feathered friends.

Thomas Jefferson (1801 – 1809) owned several mockingbirds. A favorite mockingbird, Dick, accompanied the president almost everywhere. Dick liked to perch on Jefferson's shoulder and he learned to take cherries and other bits of fruit from the president's lips. Being a true mockingbird, Dick learned to copy the sounds of other birds and animals. He could actually meow like a cat and bark like a dog! The clever bird even learned to accompany the President as Jefferson played the violin. At the end of the day, Dick would follow the President up the stairs to bed. He would hop behind President Jefferson, one step at a time, and then sweetly sing his master to sleep.

Here's a history question for you – what is our national bird? Did you answer Eagle? Good for you! James Buchanan (1857 – 1861) received not one, but two bald eagles from a friend. The eagles enjoyed their lives at Buchanan's home in Pennsylvania as they leisurely strolled around the grounds. The birds slept in twin cages at night on the back porch. They seemed perfectly happy with their home so they remained in Pennsylvania while Buchanan served as President.

Andrew Jackson (1829 – 1837) was from Tennessee and took pride in being a rugged, plainspoken politician. The President had a parrot named Poll. When Andrew Jackson died, Poll attended the funeral. Well, it seems that Poll screamed out words that should not have been repeated (obviously words he had learned from his rugged master) and the bird had to be taken outside!

James and Dolley Madison (1807 – 1817) shared the
White House with a brightly colored macaw or parrot. As
the British invaded Washington during the War of 1812,
Dolley quickly rescued two very important things from
the Presidential home. Some say that she saved a copy of
the Declaration of Independence and the family's parrot.
Others say that she saved a portrait of George
Washington and the family's parrot. In other words . . .
we know that the parrot was important to Mrs. Madison!

President William McKinley's (1897 – 1901) pet parrot
was named Washington Post. This parrot was quite a
charmer. When ladies walked by, he would squawk, "Oh,
look at all the pretty girls." Washington Post could sing
almost any song. The President would start a song by
singing a few lines and Washington Post would join
right in. He could sing *Yankee Doodle* and lots of other
patriotic songs!

Theodore Roosevelt's children (1901 – 1909) enjoyed several birds including a blue macaw named Eli Yale that loved to eat coffee grounds. They also provided a home for a barn owl, a hen, and a one-legged rooster. The children were thoughtful and made a crutch for their one-legged pet, but the rooster preferred hopping around on one leg and got along just fine!

Many pets occupied the White House with President Calvin Coolidge (1923 – 1929) and his wife Grace. Their mynah bird enjoyed sitting on top of the maid's head as she dusted and cleaned the presidential mansion. That's what I call a real feather duster . . .

Now here's a clue . . . what other animal made a great "neigh" — bor to the people in Washington, D.C.?

Oh, you're sooooooo clever . . . did you guess . . .

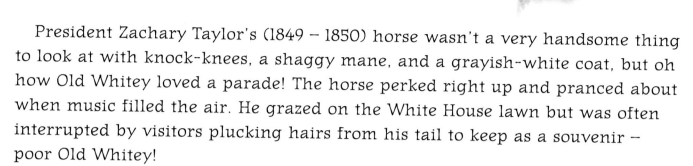

HORSES

President Zachary Taylor's (1849 – 1850) horse wasn't a very handsome thing to look at with knock-knees, a shaggy mane, and a grayish-white coat, but oh how Old Whitey loved a parade! The horse perked right up and pranced about when music filled the air. He grazed on the White House lawn but was often interrupted by visitors plucking hairs from his tail to keep as a souvenir – poor Old Whitey!

As a father, Abraham Lincoln (1861 – 1865) allowed his sons to have lots of pets. Tad and Willie Lincoln could often be seen riding their pet ponies around Washington. They even dressed in military capes and rode out with their father as he reviewed the troops.

Today a statue stands by the White House elevator to remind visitors of a very special pony. Theodore Roosevelt's pony, Algonquin, has become quite famous. Young Archie Roosevelt was sick with the measles and two of his brothers thought that a visit from Algonquin would make him feel better. They loaded the pony onto the elevator and then trotted him right down the hall to Archie's room! Everything was going fine until Algonquin noticed his reflection in the elevator's mirror. The pony liked what he saw and wanted to stay on the elevator. Luckily Kermit and Quentin Roosevelt finally convinced the pony to follow them. Some people say that you can still see an impression of Algonquin's hoof in the floor.

Algonquin the pony had a mischievous streak . . . he liked to sneak up behind unsuspecting people and nudge them with his cold nose. But Algonquin was also kind-hearted. He could often be seen galloping around the White House lawn with one of the Roosevelt's dogs sitting on his back. What a sight this must have been!

(By now you've probably realized that Theodore Roosevelt's family had *lots* of animals.)

President John F. Kennedy's (1961 – 1963) daughter had a pony named Macaroni. Macaroni enjoyed taking Caroline for a ride around the White House or sometimes the pony wandered around freely on the grounds. President Kennedy just happened to look up one day and noticed that Macaroni was looking at him through the window. Being a polite host, the president opened the window and asked if Macaroni would like to come inside. The pony just looked at the President and then turned and walked away.

Another pony, Leprechaun, loved to eat sugar cubes. One day, Leprechaun figured out that the President pulled these tasty treats from the pockets of his pants. The pony decided to nudge his master for more sugar. He pushed a little too hard and President Kennedy fell backward to the ground. The President laughed – it looked as if he was being eaten by a horse!

Okay, we've covered cats, dogs, birds and horses. What other pets lived at the White House? You're not going to believe this . . .

Would you have guessed . . . GOATS

The Lincoln family (1861 – 1865) shared their home with a pair of goats named Nanny and Nanko. The goats were regularly seen throughout the White House – often climbing onto beds to rest. Young Tad Lincoln even hitched the animals to a chair and raced up and down the hallways of the great mansion.

The president seemed to love the pets too. He once surprised everyone by giving the goats and Tad a ride in his carriage. It was funny to see the President of the United States riding through the streets with a pair of goats!

Benjamin Harrison's (1889 – 1893) grandchildren were allowed to have lots of animals, but one of the most famous Harrison pets was a goat named Old Whiskers. The children loved to hitch him to a cart and ride around the grounds. One day the children were enjoying a peaceful ride through the White House grounds when the ornery old goat decided to dash through the entrance gates. President Harrison chased after the group, holding onto his top hat and waving his walking cane, but Old Whiskers didn't stop. The people of Washington were surprised to see their distinguished President all out of breath and chasing a runaway goat cart! Finally the goat stopped and followed President Harrison back home.

On the next pages you'll see some really unusual pets . . .

Sheep

During World War I, President Woodrow Wilson (1913 – 1921) allowed sheep to "mow" the grass on the White House lawn. Sheep will graze very neatly so it looked like the grass had been mowed.

The herd included a ram named Old Ike. It seems that Old Ike had one bad habit – he liked to chew tobacco! He loved tobacco and often picked up cigar stubs to chew on. Old Ike was quite a sight with a wad of tobacco clenched in his teeth and tobacco juice trickling down his chin.

Cows

Andrew Johnson (1865 – 1869) brought two cows to live with him in Washington. Johnson's daughter, Martha, got up early each morning and milked the cows.

President William Howard Taft (1909 – 1913) was the largest president — he even had to have a bathtub built just for him — he was so big! Obviously President Taft liked to eat. A cow named Pauline was brought to the White House so the president could enjoy plenty of fresh milk and butter. The cow's milk was so tasty that Taft hired a man whose only job was to care for Pauline.

Opossums

Mr. Reciprocity and Mr. Protection were opossums belonging to Benjamin Harrison (1889 – 1893). Aren't these funny names for pets — what could they mean?

Another famous opossum belonged to Herbert Hoover (1929 – 1933). The opossum was found on the White House grounds and the President's picture appeared in the newspaper with his little friend. A high school noticed the picture and decided that this must be their missing team mascot which happened to be an opossum. They traveled to Washington and convinced President Hoover that their team would surely have bad luck without a mascot, so the president gave the opossum to the school. Maybe the little animal did bring good luck — the school's baseball team made it all the way to the state championship!

Raccoons

A favorite pet for Calvin Coolidge (1923 – 1929) was a raccoon named Rebecca. The President walked Rebecca on a leash as he strolled the grounds. He built a house just for her and once he even sent a limousine to pick up the special raccoon!

Mice

Andrew Johnson (1865 – 1869) was very lonely while at the White House. One night he noticed some mice scurrying about the mansion. He befriended the little creatures by setting out a basket for them to sleep in and he made sure that they had plenty of food and water each night.

Deer

At least three of our Presidents had a fondness for deer. Thomas Jefferson trained a herd of deer to eat corn right out of his pockets and after watching the movie Bambi, the Kennedy family briefly added deer to their pet collection. Gerald Ford's family bottle-fed a deer named Flag while staying at Camp David.

Tigers

President Martin Van Buren (1837 – 1841) received a pair of tiger cubs as a gift from a sultan. Congress decided that the best place to keep them was in a zoo, not the White House.

Snakes

The family of Theodore Roosevelt has been mentioned many times – but they had MANY animals. Young Quentin Roosevelt was so excited over his new snakes, that he burst right in the West Oval Office to show his dad. Unfortunately, President Roosevelt was in the middle of an important meeting and Quentin just happened to drop all four snakes onto the table. The Senators and party officials scattered every which way!

The President's daughter, Alice, owned a green garter snake named Emily Spinach. This name was most appropriate for it was as green as spinach and as thin as the family's Aunt Emily. Many people did not like the idea of a snake in the White House and Emily Spinach eventually died under suspicious circumstances. Now what could have happened to Emily Spinach?

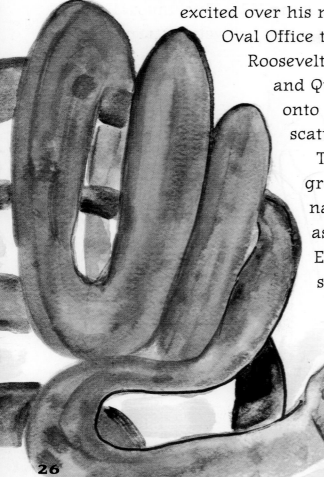

Elephants

President James Buchanan (1857 – 1861) was given a herd of elephants from the king of Siam. Obviously the White House was no place for an elephant herd, so he donated them to the zoo.

Alligators

Herbert Hoover's (1929 – 1933) son Allan had two pet alligators. Sometimes the alligators were kept in the mansion's bathtub, but sometimes they were allowed to wander around the White House!

An alligator was given to John Quincy Adams (1825 – 1829) by Marquis de Lafayette. The reptile lived at the White House while Lafayette toured America during 1825. This unusual pet lived in the East Room for several months, but when Lafayette returned to France, the alligator went with him.

Bears

Thomas Jefferson (1801-1809) was presented several grizzly bears. Lewis and Clark had been sent to explore the West and the bears were gifts from this trip. President Jefferson was amazed by these wild creatures and built a special cage for them on the White House grounds. He even took them from their cage from time to time and paraded them around in the garden.

The Theodore Roosevelt (1901 –1909) family had a small bear named Jonathan Edwards. (Of course they did, they had just about every animal that's been mentioned!) President Theodore or "Teddy" Roosevelt became famous for many things, but all through the years people have remembered him for an act of kindness shown to a small bear while hunting. One day he and a group of men came across a small bear cub. The men thought that the President would want to shoot the bear, but instead, Teddy Roosevelt laid down his rifle and told the men to let it go free. The story of the President's kindness appeared in the newspaper. A man and his wife decided to sew a soft cuddly bear to sell in their shop. They called it "Teddy's Bear." Today you can find Teddy Bears for sale everywhere!

Wow — you've just read about a lot of animals . . . but there's more!

There were also lizards, hamsters, guinea pigs, rats, rabbits, a baboon and squirrels (even a flying squirrel) . . .

a goose, turkeys, an owl, and fish . . .

pigs, a badger, a hyena, a donkey, an antelope, and a pigmy hippo . . .

a wallaby (small kangaroo), a bobcat, a jaguar, a pair of lion cubs, and silkworms.

Yes, even silkworms. Louisa Adams (wife of John Quincy Adams) reared silkworms while living in Washington. Mrs. Adams spun the silk from the cocoons of the special caterpillars and she actually made enough silk to create several of her gowns.

Most of the wild animals mentioned were donated to zoos but many of these animals were actually kept as pets.

Hundreds of pets have roamed the halls and the grounds of the White House. They have provided the First Families with hours of fun, excitement, comfort, and loyal companionship . . .

They have accompanied the Presidents while traveling, they have slept at their master's bedside, and they have snuggled in laps — wanting only one thing in return . . . love.

It's not easy being President of the United States — aren't you glad our leaders had such devoted friends?

A very wise man named Immanuel Kant once said,

A man must practice kindness toward animals,
for he who is cruel to animals becomes hard also
in his dealings with men. We can judge the heart
of a man by his treatment of animals.

Maybe this explains why so many of the men
mentioned in this book were chosen to serve
in our country's highest office . . .

What do you think?

Author's Page

Jackie, Alice, and Jennie have *many* animal stories of their own. Jackie and her husband Hal, a veterinarian, raised their family on a cattle farm. Her sons Brooks, Andy, and Ralph had many interesting animals while growing up. The favorites were their horses, War Paint, Macaroni, and Spinning Wheel. They also loved their dogs . . . Lobo, Tallulah, Chap, and Pal who helped round up the cows.

Alice and her husband Tim currently share their home with three fluffy cats and seven very active dogs. While they've never had alligators, lions, or elephants (some of the unusual pets mentioned in this book), Alice and Tim have provided room for many cats and dogs in need of a home and lots of love. The couple enjoys watching animals visit their yard — a variety of birds, ducks, rabbits, red fox, squirrels (even a white squirrel), opossums, and raccoons pass through the yard all during the year.

Jennie's three boys, Marty, Mitch and John had lots of pets. Each son seemed to have a favorite — Marty loved Nosy the Beagle, Mitch raised two special goats, and a Chocolate Lab named R.J. belonged to John.

Former First Lady Hillary Clinton made the following comments about family pets: *When we moved to Washington from Little Rock, we brought our family traditions, favorite pictures, and personal mementos to make the White House feel more comfortable. But it wasn't until Socks arrived with his toy mouse and Buddy walked in with his rawhide bone that this house became a home. Pets have a way of doing that.* WE AGREE!

First Lady Laura Bush also discussed the special role that pets have played in the lives of our First Families: *Our animals have been a great source of comfort to us . . . They are a great amusement and distraction but they also make the White House home for us.* WE AGREE!

We hope that you have also been lucky enough to have special pets in your life and we truly hope you enjoy our book!

Jackie, Alice, and Jennie